A Different Kind of Christmas
Children's Leader Guide

A Different Kind of Christmas: Living and Giving Like Jesus

An Advent Program
by Mike Slaughter

Book: Christmas Is Not Your Birthday
In five short, engaging chapters, readers are inspired to approach Christmas differently and to be transformed in the process.
978-1-4267-2735-1

DVD With Leader Guide
Video programs about ten to fifteen minutes each to accompany and complement the book, one video for each of the five chapters. Leader guide contains everything a leader needs to organize and run a five-session Advent study based on the book and videos, including discussion questions, activities, and flexible session lengths and formats.
978-1-4267-5354-1

Devotional Book: Devotions for the Season
Five weeks of devotional readings for program participants. Each reading includes Scripture, a brief story or meditation, and a prayer.
978-1-4267-5360-2

Youth Study Edition
A five-session Advent study for youth in support of the program. Written in a style and approach to inspire youth. Includes leader helps.
978-1-4267-5361-9

Children's Leader Guide
Complete lesson plans for a five-session Advent study for younger and older children, including activities and handouts.
978-1-4267-5362-6

Mike Slaughter's

A Different Kind of Christmas

Children's Leader Guide

by Sally Hoelscher

Abingdon Press
Nashville

Mike Slaughter's
A Different Kind of Christmas:
Children's Leader Guide
by Sally Hoelscher

Scripture quotations marked CEB are from the Common English Bible, © Copyright 2010 by Common English Bible, and are used by permission.

This book is printed on acid-free, elemental chlorine-free paper.

ISBN 978-1-4267-5362-6

12 13 14 15 16 17 18 19 20 —10 9 8 7 6 5 4 3 2 1

MANUFACTURED IN THE UNITED STATES OF AMERICA

CONTENTS

Invitation

You Are Invited to a
Birthday Party
for Jesus!

Please join us on

_____

at _____.

As a present for Jesus,
please bring a gift to

_____.

Items requested:

_____

_____

_____

_____

_____

_____

Suggestions for an All-church Program

In his book *A Different Kind of Christmas: Living and Giving Like Jesus,* author Mike Slaughter looks at the celebration of Christmas and suggests ways to bring the focus of the season back to the reason we celebrate. Mike Slaughter encourages us to examine our Christmas celebrations and to develop new Christmas traditions that focus on relationships and service.

A churchwide Advent program for all ages will help people come to a deeper understanding of why we celebrate Christmas and will invite families to explore ways to keep Jesus as the focus of their Christmas celebrations. It will offer opportunities for learning, intergenerational projects and activities, and reaching out in service to the community.

Resources for the Churchwide Study

Adults
Christmas Is Not Your Birthday—Book

A Different Kind of Christmas: DVD With Leader Guide—Videos

A Different Kind of Christmas: A Season of Devotions—Devotional Book

Youth
A Different Kind of Christmas: Youth Study Edition

Children
A Different Kind of Christmas: Children's Leader Guide

Schedule
Many churches have weeknight programs that include an evening meal; an intergenerational gathering time; and classes for children, youth, and adults. The following schedule illustrates one way to organize a weeknight program.

5:30 PM	Meal
6:00 PM	Intergenerational gathering introducing Bible characters and places for the lesson. This time may include presentations, skits, music, and opening or closing prayers.
6:15 PM–8:45 PM	Classes for children, youth, and adults.

Churches may want to do the Advent study as a Sunday school program. This setting would be similar to the weeknight setting. The following schedule takes into account a shorter class time. which is the norm for Sunday morning programs.

10 minutes	Intergenerational gathering
45 minutes	Classes for children, youth, and adults

Choose a schedule that works best for your congregation and its existing Christian education programs.

Activity Suggestions

Birthday Party for Jesus
An all-church party would be a good kick-off or wrap-up event. Take the opportunity to collect items as gifts for a local organization. Items for young children would be especially appropriate. Possible ideas include: children's books for a hospital library, baby supplies for a shelter, or school supplies for an elementary school.

All-church Food Drive
Lesson 1 has instructions for the children to organize a food drive and invite the entire church to participate. The food drive would last all five weeks of the study.

Service Projects
In Lesson 4, children will brainstorm ideas for a class service project. This idea could be expanded to become a churchwide service project. Alternatively, each age group could plan a service project and invite the whole church to participate.

1 Expect a Miracle

<table>
<tr><td>

Objectives

The children will
- hear Isaiah 7:14 and 9:6-7;
- discover that Isaiah foretold Jesus' birth many years before it happened;
- learn how God sent Jesus to be Immanuel, God with us;
- explore what it means to view Christmas as a celebration of God present in our lives.

</td><td>

Bible Story

Isaiah's Prophecy: Isaiah 7:14, 9:6-7

Bible Verse

Therefore the Lord will give you a sign. The young woman is pregnant and is about to give birth to a son and she will name him Immanuel. (Isaiah 7:14 CEB)

</td></tr>
</table>

Focus for the Teacher

A People in Need of Hope

Isaiah's message of a promised Messiah was delivered to people who were in need of just such a message of hope. Isaiah lived about 500 years after God had delivered the Israelites from slavery in Egypt. Many of the Israelite people had failed to put their trust in God and had begun worshiping other gods. The people were also looking for alliances with other countries to protect them instead of putting their trust in God. This was a time of social injustice, exploitation of the poor, and corruption of political and religious leaders. Do these issues sound familiar? Many of the issues facing the Israelites are ones we continue to struggle with today.

The Bible Verse

Many years before Jesus' birth, the prophet Isaiah told of God's promise to send a savior. "Therefore the Lord will give you a sign. The young woman is pregnant and is about to give birth to a son and she will name him Immanuel" (Isaiah 7:14 CEB).

Immanuel means *God is with us*. The birth of Jesus fulfilled a promise God had made. Through the words of the prophet Isaiah, God had promised to send a savior. God kept that promise by sending Jesus, God's own Son.

> As you teach, let the enthusiasm of the children remind you that *God is with us.*

Children and Christmas

Christmas is an exciting time to teach children. We may think children only look forward to Christmas because of the presents they will receive, but it is much more than that. The Christmas story is a familiar one to most children. Children like learning about the Christmas story and they enjoy celebrating Christmas. When given encouragement and opportunity, children are very generous and like to be helpers. Isaiah 11:6 (CEB) tells us that "a little child will lead them." As you teach, let the enthusiasm of the children remind you that, as promised, God is with us.

Explore Interest Groups

Be sure that adult leaders are waiting when the first child arrives. Greet and welcome each child. Get the child involved in an activity that interests him or her and introduces the theme for the day's activities.

Hidden Picture

- Invite the children to choose one color to color all the spaces that have a dot, and then choose another color to color the remaining spaces.
- **Say**: The finished picture will reveal another name for Jesus.

Discover the Message

- **Say:** Isaiah was a prophet who lived about 700 years before Jesus was born.
- Ask: Do you know what a prophet is?
- **Say**: A prophet is one who delivers messages for God. Isaiah had a special message to deliver about Jesus' birth.
- Give the children copies of Discover the Message and encourage them to complete the puzzle.
- Have the children look up the Bible verse to check their answers.

Therefore, the Lord will give you a sign. The young woman is pregnant and is about to give birth to a son, and she will name him Immanuel. (Isaiah 7:14 CEB)

Ordinary People Collage

- Show the children the mural paper and point out the title you have written at the top.
- Invite the children to look through the magazine pages and cut out pictures of people.
- Have the children glue the pictures they find onto the mural paper.
- **Say:** During our Bible story time today, we are going to discuss how God uses ordinary people to do amazing things.

Prepare
✓ Photocopy Hidden Picture (page 18) for each child.

✓ Provide crayons or markers.

Prepare
✓ Photocopy Discover the Message (page 19) for each child.

✓ Provide a Bible and pencils or crayons.

Prepare
✓ Provide mural paper, scissors, glue, and old magazines.

✓ Cut a large piece of mural paper. At the top of the paper write the words "Ordinary People."

✓ Go through the magazines and tear out pages with pictures of people. Try to find pictures that show a diversity of ages, genders, and cultures.

Prepare

✓ Provide a Nativity set, along with fabric pieces of varying sizes, rubber bands, yarn, string and scissors, paper and markers.

✓ Note: There are many different styles of Nativity sets. If possible, choose one with individual figures that include: Mary, Joseph, baby Jesus, an angel, shepherds, sheep, and wise men.

✓ Provide images of one or more of the following works by the artists Christo and Jean Claude: The Pont Neuf Wrapped, Wrapped Reichstag, and Wrapped Trees. Search online or in the library for images.

✓ Arrange a place to display the final project where it can be seen by others in your church.

Prepare

✓ Provide two mixing bowls, large spoons for stirring, serving bowls (one bowl for each small group), cutting boards, table knives or plastic knives, colander, can opener, canned mandarin oranges, canned pineapple, fresh strawberries, and bananas. You may substitute other varieties of fruit as desired.

Transformative Art

- Show the children the images of Christo and Jean Claude's art.

- **Say:** These pictures show some of the works of two artists named Christo and Jean Claude. These two artists are famous for huge outdoor art projects, which temporarily change or transform objects and helps people look at them a new way. Notice that the original objects are still recognizable in their transformed state.

- Ask: Imagine if you walked by a building every day, and then one day it was completely covered in fabric! What do you think you would do?

- Invite the children to use the materials you have provided to wrap the pieces of the Nativity set.

- **Say:** After we use your artwork during our Bible Story time today, we will put it on display so other people can look at it over the next few weeks. We will unwrap some pieces each week so your artwork will continue to change or transform.

- Have the children make a sign that says "Nativity Wrapped" to display next to their artwork. Have the children sign their names.

Make Fruit Salad for Later

- Have the children wash their hands.

- Have the children use the table knives or plastic knives to cut the stems off the strawberries and cut the strawberries into fourths.

- Have the children peel the bananas and use the table knives or plastic knives to slice the bananas.

- Have the children place the colander over one of the bowls. Have the children use the can opener to open the cans of fruit and place the fruit in the colander to drain.

- Have the children place all of the fruit into the empty bowl. Have the children take turns gently stirring the fruit until it is well mixed.

- **Say:** That looks good enough to eat! However, we are going to wait until later to eat the fruit salad.

- Have the children divide the fruit salad evenly among the serving bowls.

- Place the fruit salad in the refrigerator to be eaten later.

Isaiah says

- **Say:** A long time ago there was a prophet named Isaiah. A prophet is someone who delivers messages from God. However, people don't always listen when a prophet speaks. Let's play a game to see how good your listening skills are. I am going to give you some directions. Do whatever I say, but only if I begin with "Isaiah says." If you don't hear me begin with "Isaiah says," then don't do whatever I am asking you to do.

- Play the game using the following or other commands:

  > Isaiah says stand up.
  > Isaiah says jump up and down.
  > Stop jumping. (Some children will probably stop jumping. Do not eliminate children who make a mistake.)
  > Isaiah says stop jumping.
  > Isaiah says turn around in a circle.
  > Touch your toes.
  > Touch your ears.
  > Isaiah says reach for the sky.
  > Isaiah says hop on one foot.
  > Isaiah says wave at your neighbor while hopping on one foot.
  > Sit down.
  > Isaiah says stop hopping and waving.
  > Isaiah says sit down.

- Continue playing as the children are interested. Let the children take turns being Isaiah and giving commands.

Isaiah's Prophecy

- In preparation for a later activity (see Large Group below), invite up to six skilled readers to help you tell today's Bible story.

- Give each child a copy of Isaiah's Prophecy (page 20) with the section to read clearly marked.

- Ask the children to practice reading their sections to themselves. Remind them that when reading aloud in front of the large group, they will need to speak loudly and slowly so people will be able to hear and understand them.

Prepare

✓ Make six photocopies of Isaiah's Prophecy (page 20).

Prepare

✓ Make plans for a food drive. Decide which organizations your food gifts will go to.

✓ Call the organization you have chosen and ask if they have any specific needs.

✓ Add the necessary information to Food Drive (page 23) and photocopy the letter for each child to take home. Write the name of your class at the bottom of the note.

✓ Arrange for information about the food drive to be shared with your congregation.

✓ Provide paper, pencils, markers, large cardboard boxes or laundry baskets, poster board, and tape.

Food Drive

- **Say:** Today we are going to organize a food drive for our entire church. After Christmas, the food we collect will be given to (name of organization) and it will be distributed to people who need it. Often we think about collecting food before Christmas, but the need for these items doesn't disappear once Christmas is over. People need to eat all year long!

- Have the children make posters to decorate the collection boxes (cardboard boxes or laundry baskets) and to hang in the hallways to promote the food drive.

- Have the children hang posters in the hallway.

- Keep a collection box in your classroom.

- Place the remaining collection boxes outside your classroom to encourage other people to bring gifts for your food drive.

Large Group

Bring all the children together into a large group to experience the Bible story. Use a bell to call the children to the large group.

Pass the Present

- Invite the children to move to the large group area. Show the children the present you have prepared.

- **Say:** Often at Christmas, we exchange presents with one another. The present I have here is for all of us. As the music plays, pass the present around the room. When the music stops, whoever has the present should hold on to it.

- Begin playing the music and have the children pass the present. Continue playing the music long enough so that every child has had an opportunity to pass the present.

- Stop the music. Let the child holding the present unwrap it and read the message to the class. If a nonreader opens the present, that person can choose an older child to read the message.

- **Say:** This is the best reason to celebrate Christmas!

Prepare
✓ Provide a Christmas music CD and a CD player.

✓ On a piece of paper write the words Jesus Is God's Gift to the World. Gift-wrap the message in a box or gift bag.

Isaiah's Prophecy

- Say: Today's Bible story is about a man named Isaiah.

- Invite some older children to find the book of Isaiah in the Bible.

- **Say:** Isaiah is in the Old Testament, which means it was written before Jesus was born. Isaiah told people about Jesus a long time before Jesus was born.

- Invite the six children who have practiced reading Isaiah's Prophecy (page 20) to share it with the class.

- Ask: How many years after Isaiah lived was Jesus born? (About 700 years.)

- **Say:** Imagine if you had to wait 700 years to celebrate Christmas! Even though they had to wait a long time, the people kept waiting and hoping. Isaiah said the baby would be called Immanuel. Immanuel is another name Jesus is sometimes called.

- Ask: What does Immanuel mean? (God with us.)

- **Say:** God sent Jesus into the world to show us a better way to live. At Christmas we celebrate that God sent Jesus to be with us and we remember God is always with us.

- Show the children the wrapped Nativity set.

Prepare
✓ Photocopy Isaiah's Prophecy (page 20) for each child to take home.

✓ Provide Bibles.

✓ Have the Nativity set the children wrapped available.

- Ask: What is this? (A Nativity set.) How does this Nativity set look different from Nativity sets you have seen before? (It is wrapped up.)

- **Say:** We are going to put your wrapped Nativity set on display in the church.

- Ask: Do you think people will stop to look at it? Why?

- **Say:** Today our whole church is beginning to talk about "A Different Kind of Christmas." Sometimes it is easy to get busy at Christmas time and forget why we are celebrating. We want to take time to remember Christmas as a celebration that God is with us!

Ordinary to Extraordinary

- Ask: Who can tell me what the word *ordinary* means? (Regular, common.) What does *extraordinary* mean? (Exceptional, beyond what is expected.)

- On the mural paper, write *Bethlehem* in the ordinary column.

- **Say:** Before Jesus' birth, Bethlehem was an ordinary town. It was not very big and was probably considered unimportant by most people. But God used Bethlehem for a special purpose.

- Ask: How did God make Bethlehem extraordinary? (God chose Bethlehem to be the birthplace of Jesus.)

- On the mural paper, write *Birthplace of Jesus* in the Extraordinary column.

- **Say:** God has a wonderful way of taking places, things, and people that might be considered ordinary and making them extraordinary. Let's look at some other examples from the story of Jesus' birth.

- List the following words one at a time in the ordinary column and discuss with the children how God made the person, place, or thing extraordinary.

- Mary (Young girl who had never been married became the mother of Jesus, God's Son)

- Joseph (Carpenter who became Jesus' earthly father)

- Manger (Feed trough for animals that became a crib for Jesus)

- Shepherds (Considered outcasts of society but were the first to be told of Jesus' birth)

- Show the children the Ordinary People Collage.

- **Say:** Earlier, some of you made a collage of people. These look like ordinary people, but we know God can use ordinary people and make them extraordinary.

- Write the word *Extra* in front of the word Ordinary on the collage.

Prepare

✓ Cut a big piece of mural paper and use a marker to divide it into three columns. At the top of the first column write *Ordinary* and at the top of the third column write *Extraordinary.* Across the middle column write *Plus God* in big letters.

✓ Display the paper where the children will be able to see it.

✓ In the same area, display the Ordinary People Collage the children made earlier.

- On the mural paper with the table, write the word *You* in the ordinary column.

- Ask: Some people might say that each of you is an ordinary child, but we know God is with each one of you. And what happens when God is with you? (You become extraordinary!)

- Write *In Many Ways* in the Extraordinary column.

- **Say:** Maybe you are extraordinary because you are really good at showing others God's love by sharing hugs. Or maybe God has given you a special talent that you can share with others. Each of you is extraordinary in your own way because God loves you.

Give Me a Sign

- **Say:** Today's Bible verse is Isaiah 7:14. Read the verse from the Bible.

- Ask: What did Isaiah say the baby's name would be? (Immanuel.)

- Teach the children sign language for *Immanuel*. Form the sign for the letter *I* with your right hand by making a fist with your pinky finger raised in the air. Bring your hand across your body from the left shoulder to the right hip. (For each of the signs in this activity, you might want to go online to see a picture of what the sign looks like.)

- Ask: What does *Immanuel* mean? (God with us.)

- Teach the children sign language for *God with us.*

- Teach the children the sign for *God*. Raise your right hand with fingers together and thumb toward you. Begin with the hand raised high as a sign of respect and bring it downward in front of you.

- Teach the children the sign for *with*. Hold both hands in a fist with the thumb to the side of the fingers, forming the sign for the letter a. Bring your hands together in front of you.

- Teach the children the sign for *us*. Form the sign for the letter *u* with your right hand by holding your index and middle fingers up together. Begin at your right shoulder and make an arc toward your left shoulder.

- Have the children practice making the four signs.

- **Say:** I am going to sign either *Immanuel* or *God with us*. If I sign *Immanuel,* you will sign *God with us* in response. If I sign *God with us* you will sign *Immanuel* in response.

- Do this several times.

Prepare
✓ Provide a Bible with a bookmark at Isaiah 7:14.

Small Groups

Divide the children into small groups. You may organize the groups around age levels (4-7, 8-11) or around readers and nonreaders. Keep the groups small, with a maximum of ten children in each group. You may need to have more than one group at each age level.

Prepare

✓ Photocopy the Prepare for Christmas strips (pages 21-22) on colored paper for each child.

✓ Provide construction paper, crayons, scissors, stickers (optional), and transparent tape.

✓ Pre-fold a piece of construction paper for each child. Fold the short edges of the paper over to meet in the middle; crease and unfold. Fold the long edges of the paper over to meet in the middle; crease and unfold.

✓ Provide the fruit salad prepared earlier, whipped topping (in a spray bottle or a carton), small bowls or cups, napkins, and spoons.

Young Children

- **Say:** We are going to make something for you to take home and use as you prepare to celebrate Christmas.

- Let each child choose a piece of construction paper you have prepared.

- Give the children scissors and have them cut from the short edges of the paper, along the fold lines, stopping at the other fold line. There should be four slits in the paper when they have finished cutting.

- Have the children fold up the paper along the long fold line, folding the flaps in to form a box.

- Have the children tape the flaps together.

- Have the children fold up each short side of the paper and fold it over the taped flaps, securing it with another piece of tape.

- Invite the children to decorate their boxes with crayons and stickers.

- Give the children one copy each of the Prepare for Christmas pages (pages 21 and 22) and a pair of scissors.

- Have the children cut apart the activity strips and place the strips in the decorated box.

- **Say:** Take your box home. Each day, take a strip out of the box and do the activity on the strip. As you finish the activities, you can use the strips to make a paper chain, adding a circle on each day. You will see your chain grow longer and longer as Christmas gets closer!

- Have the children help pass out bowls, napkins, and spoons. Serve the fruit salad, reminding the children not to eat until everyone has been served.

- **Say:** This fruit salad looks really good! Thank you to those who helped make it. We have a special treat to make the fruit salad extraordinary.

- Let the children add a small amount of whipped topping to their fruit salad. Enjoy the snack together.

- **Say:** When you go home today, share with your family what you've learned about Jesus' name, Immanuel, which means *God is with us.*

- Pray: Thank you, God, for our time together and for fruit salad. As we prepare to celebrate Christmas, help us remember the good news that you are with us. Amen.

- Remind the children to take a note home about the food drive.

A Different Kind of Christmas: Children's Leader Guide

Older Children

- **Say:** We are going to make something for you to take home and use as you prepare to celebrate Christmas.

- Invite each child to choose a piece of construction paper.

- Have the children fold the short edges of the paper over to meet in the middle. Have the children crease the edges and then unfold the paper.

- Have the children fold the long edges of the paper over to meet in the middle. Have the children crease the edges and then unfold the paper.

- Give the children a pair of scissors and have them cut from the short edges of the paper, along the fold lines, stopping at the other fold line. There should be four slits in the paper when they have finished cutting.

- Have the children fold up the paper along the long fold line, folding the flaps in to form a box, and taping the flaps together.

- Have the children fold up each short side of the paper and fold it over the taped flaps, securing it with another piece of tape.

- Invite the children to decorate their boxes with markers.

- Give the children one copy each of the Prepare for Christmas pages (pages 21 and 22) and a pair of scissors.

- Have the children cut apart the activity strips and place the strips in the decorated box.

- **Say:** Take your box home and place it somewhere you will see it every day. Each day, take a strip out of the box and do the activity on the strip. As you complete the activities, you can use the strips to make a paper chain, adding a circle each day. You will see your chain grow longer and longer as it gets closer to Christmas!

- Have the children help pass out bowls, mapkins, and spoons. Serve each child some fruit salad, reminding them not to eat until everyone has been served.

- **Say:** This fruit salad looks really good! Thank you to those who helped make it. We have a special treat to make the fruit salad extraordinary.

- Let the children add a small amount of whipped topping to their fruit salad. Enjoy the snack together.

- Enjoy the snack together.

Prepare

✓ Photocopy the Prepare for Christmas strips (pages 21-22) on colored paper for each child.

✓ Provide construction paper, markers, scissors, stickers, and transparent tape.

✓ Provide whipped topping (in a spray bottle or a carton), small bowls or cups, napkins, and spoons for eating the fruit salad.

Hidden Picture

Color all the spaces that have a dot one color, and color all the spaces that are empty a different color.
Your coloring will reveal another name for Jesus.

Discover the Message

In the puzzle below, cross out the following letters each time they appear: C, J, K, Q, X, and Z.

Write the remaining letters on the blanks below.

Check your answer by looking up Isaiah 7:14 CEB.

T X H C E Q C Z R E J F O Q R K E C T

H X E J L O Q R D W I K L X L G I V Z

E Y O K U A K J S I Q Z G N T H C E Z

Y O J U X N Q G C W O J X M J A N I S

C P J R K E G K Q N A J N T A Q N C D

I S X A B O C U T K T O G I C V E B I

Q R T C H T O C A S O Q Q N A N Z D J

S H Q X E W I J L X L N A K M E H Z I

J M I M X M C A N U J Q E K L C K J X

_____, ___ ____ ____ ____ ___ _ ____. ___ _____

_____ __ _____ ___ __ _____ __ ____ _____ __ _

___, ___ ___ ____ ____ ___ _____. (Isaiah 7:14 CEB)

Isaiah's Prophecy

Many years ago there lived a prophet named Isaiah. A prophet is a person who speaks for God. Isaiah delivered many messages from God during his lifetime.

At the time Isaiah was alive, God's people were not very happy. People were not always treated fairly. Some people were forgetting to trust God and were worshiping other gods.

One of the messages Isaiah delivered from God was a message of hope. Isaiah told of a person who would come to lead God's people and be their savior. He said that a young woman would have a baby and the baby would be named Immanuel, which means *God is with us*.

Isaiah told the people what this savior would be like. Isaiah said this leader would be called Wonderful Counselor, Mighty God, Everlasting Father, and Prince of Peace. These names describe a leader who is wise, understanding, strong, caring, and a builder of peace.

Over 700 years after Isaiah told God's people about the promised Savior, Jesus was born. That's a long time to wait! Even though it took a long time, God kept the promise to send a savior. God sent Jesus to be born as a baby, just as the prophet Isaiah had foretold.

One of Jesus' names is Immanuel. Jesus' birth shows us that God will always be with us. When we celebrate Christmas we remember the wonderful gift God gave the world when Jesus was born.

Based on Isaiah 7:14 and 9:6-7.

Prepare for Christmas - 1

Dance joyfully today! Thank God for the ability to move.

An angel delivered a message to Mary before Jesus was born. With your family, read Luke 1:26-38. Then write or draw a message about Christmas on a piece of paper and deliver it to someone.

Count the number of water faucets in your house. Thank God for clean water.

Read a Christmas book today.

Try to use only kind words all day today.

Mary and Joseph journeyed to Bethlehem. With your family, read Luke 2:1-7.

With your family, discuss how you celebrate Christmas. Are there any traditions you would like to change?

Write or draw a thank-you note to someone who has done something nice for you.

Draw a picture for Jesus. Hang it up in your room.

Tell someone the story of Christmas in your own words.

Mary and Joseph were homeless when Jesus was born. Say a prayer for those who are homeless this Christmas.

Go through your closet and find clothes that no longer fit. With your family, think of a place to send your clothes where they will be used.

Prepare for Christmas - 2

Smile at everyone you see today. Let them think you are up to something!

Find some objects that remind you of Jesus. Use them to decorate a special "Christmas spot" on a windowsill or a table.

Make a poster announcing the upcoming celebration of Jesus' birthday.

Secretly do something nice for each person in your family today.

Ask a family member to tell you about the day you were born.

Sing a Christmas carol today.

Read Isaiah 9:6-7 with your family. Isaiah said these words many years before Jesus was born.

Take a walk outside and thank God for nature.

With your family, talk about why some people might be sad at Christmas. Say a prayer asking God to be with people who are sad.

Put some birdseed or popcorn in your yard as a Christmas present for the birds.

Jesus is sometimes called the Light of the World. Count the number of light bulbs in your house. Thank God for light.

An angel spoke to Joseph in a dream. With your family, read Matthew 1:18-24. Tell your family about a dream you have had.

Ask someone who is older than you to tell you their favorite Christmas memory.

Food Drive

As our church is studying about "A Different Kind of Christmas," we will be collecting nonperishable food items. After Christmas we will give these items as gifts to

_____.

The need for food does not end with Christmas!
Items that are particularly needed at this time include

_____

_____

_____

_____

_____

We invite you to bring items throughout the time of this study and place them
in the collection boxes located throughout the church.
Thank you for helping us share God's love with others.

With gratitude,

_____

2 Perfectly Loved by God

Objectives

The children will
- hear Luke 1:26-33;
- learn how God chose Mary to be Jesus' mother;
- discover that they have been chosen as God's children;
- explore ways to remember God's love and celebrate Christmas even when life does not go smoothly.

Bible Story

Gabriel and Mary: Luke 1:26-33

Bible Verse

When the angel came to [Mary] he said, "Rejoice, favored one! The Lord is with you!" (Luke 1:28 CEB)

Focus for the Teacher

Do Not Be Afraid

The New Testament contains five accounts of angels telling someone not to be afraid. Three of these accounts are connected with announcements of Jesus' birth: to Joseph (Matthew 1:20), to Mary (Luke 1:30), and to the shepherds (Luke 2:10). The other two occurrences are found in the announcement to Zechariah of John the Baptist's upcoming birth (Luke 1:13) and in the reassurance to the women at the empty tomb following Jesus' resurrection (Matthew 28:5).

The frequency with which angels spoke the reassuring phrase "Do not be afraid," makes one wonder why it was necessary! Were angels terrifying to behold, such that their appearance required reassurance? Or did the appearance of an angel usually signify such an important pronouncement, and possibly a life-altering event, that their presence automatically elicited a response of fear? Or was it, perhaps, a combination of these two?

For Mary, her encounter with the angel Gabriel certainly qualified as a life-changing event. Life as she knew it was about to change dramatically. Had she known how much, she might have been even more afraid.

The Bible Verse

The angel told Mary that she had found favor with God. Many assume that those who are blessed by God will enjoy wealth and good health. Mary's blessing, however, was that she would have a child out of wedlock. It is unlikely that this news made Mary's life easier, even though she was carrying God's Son.

Children and Christmas

Children can relate to the experience of being surprised and not having things happen as they expected or wanted them to. After all, as children they are not the ones making the rules and decisions.

Sometimes society conveys the message that one is always supposed to be happy and joyful at Christmas. The truth is that at Christmastime we experience a range of feelings, just as we do at other times of the year. Use today's lesson as an opportunity to let children know God is with them no matter what they are feeling.

Explore Interest Groups

Be sure that adult leaders are waiting when the first child arrives. Greet and welcome each child. Get the children involved in an activity that interests them and introduces the theme for the day's activities.

Bible Verse Puzzle

- **Say:** In our Bible story today, we will hear about an angel appearing to Mary to tell her she was going to have a baby.

- **Ask:** Who was that baby? (Jesus.) Do you think this message might have surprised Mary?

- **Say:** The angel told Mary not to be afraid. This puzzle will tell you something else the angel said to Mary.

- Give the children copies of A Message for Mary (page 32) and invite them to complete the puzzle.

Prepare

✓ Photocopy A Message for Mary (page 32) for each child.

✓ Provide Bibles and pencils.

Food Collection Update

- As each child arrives, have him or her place any food items they brought in the collection box.

- Have the children check the food collection boxes that you placed in other areas of the building and bring the collected food to your classroom, leaving the boxes in place.

- Have the children count the number of items collected. Let them know you will ask them to report on the food drive during large group time.

- **Say:** We will leave the collection boxes in place and keep encouraging people to bring in food items. Sharing food with others is one way we can show God's love.

Prepare

✓ Place near the door the food collection container that you decorated last week.

✓ Provide copies of the Food Drive letter (page 23) to give children who did not get one last week.

Make Cards to Share

- **Say:** We think of Christmas as a happy time, and it is. But even at Christmastime there are people who are sad for many reasons. Today we are going to make cards to share with people who might need some extra cheer. The cards will be delivered to people who could use a reminder that someone is thinking about them. The cards we make will also remind them that God is with them no matter how they are feeling.

- Give each child a piece of paper, and ask the children to bring the short sides together and fold the paper in half to make a card.

- Have the children use scissors to make a 1 to 2-inch cut in the card,

Prepare

✓ Photocopy Christmas Card Messages (page 33).

✓ Provide white or colored paper, construction paper, crayons, markers, and scissors.

✓ Arrange with your pastor or others to take the cards the children make and distribute them to people in the hospital or people who need to know you are thinking of them.

beginning at the folded edge. The cut can be anywhere along the edge of the paper but should not be too close to the top or bottom of the card.

- Have the children fold back the flaps created by the cut to form a triangle, then crease the folds.

- Have the children unfold the flaps, turn the card over, and fold and unfold the flaps on the other side.

- Have the children open the card like a tent, push the triangles toward the inside, reclose the card, and press firmly.

- Show the children how, when the card is opened, it resembles a mouth.

- Invite the children to choose a piece of construction paper and fold it in half, short sides together, to make a card.

- Have the children glue the paper card into the construction paper card, taking care not to glue the pop-up area.

- Encourage the children to draw a silly face around the pop-up mouth on the inside of the card.

- Have the children cut out one or more word bubbles from the Christmas Card Messages (page 33) and glue these on the inside of the card.

- Have the children decorate the front of the card and sign their name.

- Tell the children who will be delivering the cards they make.

- **Say:** The cards you have made are going to make some people smile this week!

Prepare

✓ Photocopy Gabriel and Mary (page 34) for each child.

Bible Story Practice

- In preparation for a later activity (see Large Group, below), invite up to seven skilled readers to help you tell today's Bible story.

- Give the children copies of Gabriel and Mary (page 34) with the section they are to read clearly marked.

- Have the children practice reading their sections.

- Tell the children that, during the Large Group activity, instead of having them come up front to read, you would like them to sit spread out among the class.

- Say: When it is your turn, stand up where you are and read your section. Remember to speak loudly and slowly so people will be able to hear and understand you.

Continue the transformation

- **Say:** Last week you transformed a Nativity set by wrapping each piece in fabric. The Nativity set has been on display in the church.

- Ask: Do you remember why we wrapped the Nativity set? (To get people to notice it. To encourage people to think about Christmas in a different way.)

- **Say:** Today we are going to transform the Nativity set again. This time we will unwrap a few of the pieces, while leaving the remaining pieces wrapped.

- Lead the children to where the wrapped Nativity set is on display.

- Have the children unwrap the figures of Mary, Joseph, and the angel.

- Ask: Do you think anyone will notice these changes?

God Loves People Who. . .

- Ask: Whom does God love? (Everyone!)

- **Say:** Absolutely! God loves each and every one of us all the time, regardless of whether we have long hair or short hair, whether we are happy or sad, and whether we have been naughty or nice. We are going to play a game to celebrate that God loves all of us.

- Have one child stand in the middle of the circle while the other children sit on chairs.

- **Say:** The person in the middle will tell us something about themselves, beginning with "God loves people who . . . " For example, if you have blue eyes you might say, "God loves people who have blue eyes." If you are eight years old you might say, "God loves people who are eight years old." Whatever is said, everyone who fits that category needs to stand up and move to a different chair. The person in the middle will try to find a seat, and the person left standing will be the next person to say "God loves people who . . ." If you are in the middle and are having trouble thinking of something to share, you can always say, "God loves everyone!" and everyone will need to move to a different chair.

- Play the game.

Prepare

✓ Arrange chairs (one less than the number of children playing the game) in a circle facing inward.

Large Group

Bring all the children together to experience the Bible story. Use a bell to call the children to the large group.

Prepare

✓ Photocopy Gabriel and Mary (page 34) for each child to take home.

✓ Provide Bibles.

Gabriel and Mary

- **Say:** Last week we talked about a man named Isaiah who lived many years before Jesus was born. Today our Bible story is about Mary, the mother of Jesus.

- Invite some older children to find the book of Luke in the Bible.

- **Say:** Our story today is from the book of Luke, which is in the New Testament. The New Testament is where we find stories about Jesus' birth, life, and ministry.

- Invite the children who have practiced reading Gabriel and Mary (see Bible Story Practice, above) to share it with the class from where they are sitting.

- Ask: Do you think when Mary woke up that morning she was expecting to be visited by an angel? How do you imagine Mary felt when Gabriel appeared? (Scared, nervous.) What do you think Mary felt when Gabriel first told her she was going to have a baby? (Surprise, shock, disbelief.)

- **Say:** The news Gabriel brought to Mary changed her life from that day forward. We can imagine that this news sometimes made Mary's life difficult.

- Ask: Can you think of a time when something happened that you weren't expecting? How did that make you feel? Allow the children time to share.

- **Say:** The good news is that, no matter what happens in life or what we are feeling, God is with us. Also, God gave us each other so we can be friends and help one another during happy times and sad times. One of the ways our class is helping people is through our food drive.

Invite the children who helped collect the food to report how much food was in the boxes so far. Talk about ways to continue encouraging people in your congregation to make gifts of food.

Remember that God Is With You

- **Say:** We are going to spend some time remembering God is with us regardless of how we are feeling. I am going to have you close your eyes while I read some statements to help you remember. After each statement I will invite you to take a deep breath and then let it out.

- Invite the children to find a comfortable sitting position and close their eyes.

- Read the following statements slowly and calmly:

Remember a time you were happy. God is with you when you are happy.

Take a deep breath . . . and let it out.

Remember a time you were excited. God is with you when you are excited.

Take a deep breath . . . and let it out.

Remember a time you were hurt. God is with you when you are hurt.

Take a deep breath . . . and let it out.

Remember a time you were angry. God is with you when you are angry.

Take a deep breath . . . and let it out.

Remember a time you were sad. God is with you when you are sad.

Take a deep breath . . . and let it out.

Remember a time you felt loved. God is with you and loves you all the time.

Take a deep breath . . . and let it out.

- Invite the children to open their eyes.

- **Say:** No matter what we are feeling, we remember and celebrate that God is with us.

The Appearing Bible Verse

- Show the children the mural paper you have displayed.

- **Say:** Here is our Bible verse for today. Let's say it together.

- When the children point out that there are no words on the paper, say: You are right! We'd better add some words.

- Invite a child to choose an index card and tape it on the mural paper over the corresponding number.

- **Say:** Now we have one word! Let's say our verse together. In places where we don't know the word yet, we will say the number.

- Point to the numbers and words as the class says them together.

- Continue to invite children to choose index cards and add words to the verse, saying the verse and numbers after each addition until the verse is complete.

- Ask: What does it mean to be a favored one? (Special.)

- **Say:** The angel called Mary "favored one" to let her know she was special to God. Each one of you is special to God also. Each of you is a favored one.

Prepare

✓ Provide a large piece of mural paper, index cards, markers, tape, and a basket or paper bag.

✓ Write the following words on the index cards, one word per card: When the angel came to Mary he said, "Rejoice, favored one! The Lord is with you!" (Luke 1:28 CEB)

✓ Number the index cards on the back side, in order from 1 to 17, then shuffle them and place them in a basket or paper bag.

✓ Tape the mural paper up where the children will be able to see it. Write the numbers 1 through 17 on the mural paper in order, spacing the numbers out to allow room for the index cards.

✓ Optional: If you are short on time, you may add more than one word at a time to the verse.

Small Groups

Divide the children into small groups. You may organize the groups around age levels (4-7, 8-11) or around readers and nonreaders. Keep the groups small, with a maximum of ten children in each group. You may need to have more than one group at each age level.

Prepare

✓ Photocopy The Gift of a Memory (page 35) for each child.

✓ Provide crayons, scissors, and stickers. Angel stickers would fit in with today's lesson, but any small sticker will do.

✓ Provide a hand-held mirror for each small group.

Young Children

- Ask: How many of you receive gifts at Christmas? How many of you give gifts at Christmas? Can you think of a gift you could give that doesn't cost anything?

- Allow the children time to share their ideas.

- Give each child a copy of The Gift of a Memory (page 35). Read aloud the paragraph at the top of the page.

- **Say:** Think about someone you really like to spend time with; it might be a family member or a friend. Now think about something you have done with this person.

- Invite the children to draw a picture about spending time together with the person they have thought of.

- Encourage the children to sign their name at the bottom of the picture.

- Have the children cut off the top part of the page.

- Have the children roll up their picture and secure it with a sticker.

- Help the children write the names of their gift recipients on the outside of the roll.

- **Say:** The next time you see this person, you can give them this gift.

- Have the children sit in a circle.

- **Say:** Earlier we talked about Mary being God's "favored one." In other words, Mary was special to God.

- Ask: Would you like to see what someone who is special to God looks like?

- Show the children the mirror.

- **Say:** Every time we look in the mirror, we see someone who is special to God. Every time we look at another person, we see someone who is special to God. We are going to take turns looking in the mirror and reminding each other we are special to God.

- Pass the mirror around the circle. As each child looks in the mirror, encourage the rest of the children to say, "_____, you are special to God."

- Pray: Loving God, we thank you for making each one of us special. Thank you for the gift of Jesus. Help us to remember you are with us always. Amen.

Older Children

- Ask: How many of you receive gifts at Christmas? How many of you give gifts at Christmas? Can you think of a gift you could give that doesn't cost anything?

- Allow the children time to share their ideas.

- Give each child a copy of The Gift of a Memory (page 35).

- Invite the children to read the paragraph at the top of the page.

- **Say:** Think about someone you really like to spend time with; it could be a family member or a friend. Now think about something you have done with this person.

- Invite the children to write a letter to the person they have thought of, reminding them of something they have done together. Encourage the children to include information about how remembering that time together makes them feel.

- Have the children sign their name at the bottom of the picture.

- Have the children cut out their letter.

- Have the children fold the letter diagonally, bringing two opposite corners together, then crease and unfold.

- Have the children fold the letter diagonally in the other direction, bringing the other two corners together, then crease and unfold.

- Have the children fold each corner of the paper in to the center. When all the corners are folded in, have the children secure the corners with a sticker.

- Have the children write the name of the letter's recipient on the outside of the letter.

- **Say:** The next time you see this person, you can give them this gift.

- Have the children sit in a circle.

- **Say:** Earlier we talked about Mary being God's "favored one." In other words, Mary was special to God.

- Ask: Would you like to see what someone who is special to God looks like?

- Show the children the mirror.

- **Say:** Every time we look in the mirror, we see someone who is special to God. Every time we look at another person, we see someone who is special to God. We are going to take turns looking in the mirror and reminding each other we are all special to God.

- Pass the mirror around the circle. As each child looks in the mirror, encourage the rest of the children to say, "_____, you are special to God."

- Pray: Loving God, we thank you for making each one of us special. Thank you for the gift of Jesus, reminding us you are with us always. Help us to remember to share your love with everyone we meet. Amen.

Prepare

✓ Photocopy The Gift of a Memory (page 35) for each child.

✓ Provide colored pencils, scissors, and stickers. Angel stickers would fit in with today's lesson, but any small sticker will do.

✓ Provide a hand-held mirror for each small group.

A Message for Mary

God sent an angel to tell Mary she was going to have a baby. Follow the directions below to discover which word to write on each line. When you are finished, read down to discover the message spoken by the angel. Look in your Bible for Luke 1:28 to check your answer.

When	drawing	the	sky	and	grass	he	liked
to	pick	one	with	many	colors	Each	time
you	hear	an	angel	you	dance	then	when
Rejoice	and	sing	came	from	God	everyone	will
see	that	it	is	fabulous	All	the	favored
said	give	the	purple	grapes	to	Mary	please

When

Forward 2 _____

Down 2 and Forward 1 _____

Down 1 _____

Forward 2 and Down 2 _____

Forward 1 _____

Up 5 _____

Back 6 and Down 5 _____

Up 2 _____

Forward 7 and Down 1 _____

Back 5 and Up 3 _____

Down 2 and Forward 3 _____

Down 1 and Back 2 _____

Up 3 _____

Forward 1 and Down 1 _____

Christmas Card Messages

At Christmas we remember that God is with us!

Never forget - God is with you always!

God sent Jesus as a reminder that God is with us!

Jesus is named Immanuel, which means God is with us!

God is with you, at Christmastime and always!

Gabriel and Mary

Based on Luke 1:26-33

God sent the angel Gabriel to Nazareth to tell Mary
she was going to have a baby.

Mary was engaged to Joseph, but she was still living
in her father's house since they weren't married yet.

Mary was a young girl, probably around twelve or thirteen years of
age. This was the age when girls got married at that time.

Gabriel told Mary she had found favor with God.
He also reminded her that God was with her.

Mary was confused by the angel's words.

The angel told Mary not to be afraid.
Gabriel said God was honoring Mary by choosing her.

Gabriel told Mary that her baby was God's Son. He said her baby
would be named Jesus and He would do many great things.

The Gift of a Memory

There are many presents we can share with people that don't cost any money at all. One such gift is to share with someone a memory of something you have done together. The person you give this gift to will have the joy of remembering time you spent together.

I remember when we

Thank you for spending time with me.

3 Outrageous Love

Objectives

The children will

- hear Luke 2:1-7;
- learn about Jesus' birth;
- discover that God loves them;
- explore ways to celebrate Christmas by showing love toward other people.

Bible Story

The Birth of Jesus: Luke 2:1-7

Bible Verse

God so loved the world that he gave his only Son, so that everyone who believes in him won't perish but will have eternal life. (John 3:16 CEB)

Focus for the Teacher

Jesus' Birth

It might seem that the birth of Jesus would warrant pages of narrative. Luke, however, tells the story in two verses. "While they were there, the time came for Mary to have her baby. She gave birth to her firstborn child, a son, wrapped him snugly, and laid him in a manger, because there was no place for them in the guestroom." (Luke 2:6-7 CEB)

Although Mary was from Nazareth, Jesus was born in Bethlehem, where the couple had traveled to register for tax purposes. Jesus' birth in Bethlehem helped fulfill a prophecy made over 700 years before His birth.

The manger Jesus was placed in was probably a feeding trough—certainly not the splendor we would imagine God's Son might have been born into!

There are many details of Jesus' birth that we are not told. Oftentimes the few details we know are enhanced and expanded upon. Regardless of the details we know or may be uncertain about, the important thing is that God loved the world enough to give us the gift of Jesus.

> When we celebrate Christmas, we are celebrating God's outrageous love for the world.

The Bible Verse

Martin Luther called John 3:16 "the gospel in miniature." The essential elements of the Gospel message are summed up in this verse: "God so loved the world that he gave his only Son, so that everyone who believes in him won't perish but will have eternal life" (John 3:16 CEB). This verse reminds us that when we celebrate Christmas, we are celebrating God's outrageous love for the world.

Children and Christmas

The Bible story for today's lesson is familiar to us. To many of us, it's just not Christmas until we hear or read these words. It is comforting to hear words that we know so well. However, we didn't become familiar with these words overnight. We recognize this story because we have heard it many times. You are giving the gift of familiarity with this story to the children you teach. By hearing the story every year, children will come to be comforted by the story of Jesus' birth—the birth of Immanuel, *God with us.*

Explore Interest Groups

Be sure that adult leaders are waiting when the first child arrives. Greet and welcome each child. Get the children involved in an activity that interests them and introduces the theme for the day's activities.

Abundant Grace

- Ask: Do you notice anything different about our room today? (There are cards everywhere.)

- Invite an older child to pick up one of the cards and read the message to the class.

- **Say:** Today we are going to be talking about God's grace. Because of grace we know that God loves us *all* the time. It doesn't matter where we are or what we do.

- Have the children work together to collect the cards spread around the room.

- Invite the children to use colored pencils and stickers to decorate the cards.

- **Say:** When we leave today, everyone will take some of these cards to help spread the message of God's grace to other people.

Prepare

✓ Photocopy Grace Messages (page 45) on white or colored cardstock. Make enough copies so that each child will be able to take home at least eight cards.

✓ Cut apart the cards and spread them all over the room. It is not necessary to hide them.

✓ Provide colored pencils and small stickers.

God's Greatest Gift

- Ask: What was the gift God gave to the world that we celebrate each year at Christmas? (Jesus.)

- Give each child a copy of God's Greatest Gift (page 46).

- Invite children who are readers to read the verse along with you.

- Have the children tear tissue paper into strips and small pieces.

- Have the children place a piece of tissue paper on the page and use a paintbrush to cover it with glue.

- **Say:** When the glue is dry, the writing on the page will show through the tissue paper.

- Have the children continue gluing tissue paper onto the page, encouraging them to overlap the pieces.

- Set the pictures aside to dry.

Prepare

✓ Photocopy God's Greatest Gift (page 46) onto cardstock for each child.

✓ Provide tissue paper in earth colors (blue, green, brown, and white), glue, empty plastic containers, and paintbrushes.

✓ Cover the work area with a protective table covering or newspapers.

✓ Place glue in each of the plastic containers, and add water to thin to the consistency of the paint.

Continue the transformation

- **Say:** Two weeks ago you transformed a Nativity set by wrapping each piece in fabric. We hope that people have seen the Nativity set and have been thinking about it.

- Ask: Do you remember which figures we unwrapped last week? (Mary, Joseph, and the angel.)

- **Say:** Today we are going to transform the Nativity set again. This time we will unwrap Jesus, while leaving the remaining pieces wrapped.

- Lead the children to where the wrapped Nativity set is on display.

- Have the children unwrap the figure of Jesus.

- Ask: Do you think anyone will notice this change?

Snowflake Hearts

- Give the children folded sheets of paper, one each, and invite them to cut along the line you have drawn.

- Have the children open up the paper to see the heart shape.

- Ask: What does this shape make you think of? (Love.)

- **Say:** Today our Bible verse tells us that God loves the entire world!

- Have the children fold the hearts in the following way:

- Bring tip of the heart up to meet the point where the top of the heart dips down.

- Fold the heart in half along the previous fold line.

- Bring the folded edges together to form a cone shape.

- Keeping the paper folded, invite the children to cut off the tip of the cone shape and cut small shapes out of each folded edge. For younger children, draw shapes along the folded edges for them to cut out.

- Invite the children to open up the heart snowflake carefully.

- Let the children enjoy making more snowflakes with different designs, as time permits.

What Does Love Look Like?

- Ask: What does love look like?

- Allow children to share their ideas.

- **Say:** These are all great images of love. There are many other ways love can be shown as well.

- Invite the children to draw pictures on the paper to answer the question.

Prepare

✓ Provide white paper, pencils, and scissors.

✓ Fold each sheet of paper in half, bringing the short sides together. On one side of the paper draw half of a heart shape, such that the middle of the heart is along the folded edge. If you have older children in your class, you can have them do these steps themselves.

Prepare

✓ Provide mural paper, tape, and markers.

✓ Cut a large sheet of mural paper. At the top of the paper write, "What does love look like?" Tape the paper on a wall where the children will be able to draw on it. Place the markers near the wall.

Food Collection Update

- As the children arrive, have them place any food items they brought in the collection box.

- Have the children check the food collection boxes in other areas of the building and bring the collected food to your classroom, leaving the boxes in place.

- Have the children count the number of items collected. Let them know you will ask them to report on the food drive during large group time.

- **Say:** We will leave the collection boxes in place and keep encouraging people to bring in food items. Sharing food with others is one way we can show God's love.

Prepare

✓ Place near the door the food collection container you decorated two weeks ago.

3:16 Geography

- Divide the children into small groups. Make sure each group includes at least one reader.

- Give each group a map, a piece of paper, and a pencil.

- Have each group use the map to make a list of sixteen countries.

- Have the groups exchange lists.

- **Say:** I am going to set the timer for 3 minutes and 16 seconds. In that time, see how many of the countries you can find. As you find the countries, check them off on your list.

- Use the timer or a clock with a second hand to give the children 3 minutes and 16 seconds to complete this activity.

- Ask: How many countries did you find?

- Have the children help each other find any countries they were unable to locate in the time allotted.

- Ask: To which of these countries was God's gift of Jesus given? (All of them.)

- **Say:** At Christmas we celebrate that Jesus was God's gift to the whole world.

Prepare

✓ Provide a world map for each group. Free world maps can be obtained at www.mapsofworld.com. [Note: Web sites are constantly changing. Although this Web site was active at the time this book was edited, we recommend before the activity that you double-check the site to verify that it is still live and that it is still appropriate for children.]

✓ Optional: Instead of maps, provide each group with a globe.

✓ Provide paper, pencils, and a timer.

Large Group

Bring all the children together to experience the Bible story. Use a bell to alert the children that large group time is beginning.

Prepare

✓ Provide a Christmas music CD and a CD player.

Prepare

✓ Provide Bibles.

Sharing Blessings

- Divide the children into two even groups. If you have an odd number of children, have an adult join one of the groups.

- Have one group of children form a circle. Tell this group they will be walking clockwise.

- Have the second group form a circle outside the first circle. Tell this group they will be walking counterclockwise.

- **Say:** When I begin playing the music, you will begin walking. When the music stops, stop walking and turn to face the person in the other circle who is next to you. When everyone has found a partner, you will then share a blessing with your partner by telling that person one thing you like about him or her.

- Play the game several times, encouraging the children to share blessings with one another each time the music stops.

- Ask: How does it make you feel when someone says something nice to you?

- **Say:** Christmas is a great time to remember to share God's love with other people.

Outrageous Love

- **Say:** Our Bible verse for today is one you might have heard before. It talks about Jesus being God's gift to the world.

- Invite some older children to look up John 3:16 and have one of the children read the verse to the class.

- Ask: Whom does God love? (The world.) Is there anyone in the world God does not love? (No.) Is there anything you can do to make God stop loving you? (No.)

- **Say:** There is absolutely nothing you can do that would make God stop loving you. Of course, because God loves us, God wants us to do the right thing. God sent Jesus into the world to show us the way to live. But even when we mess up, God still loves us! The way God loves us is amazing! Some would call it outrageous love because it is so extraordinary.

- **Say:** I am going to name some people God loves. After each group of people I name, I want you to shout, "Outrageous love!"

- Read the following statements or some of your own, pausing after each statement for the children to respond:

  God loves children! (Outrageous love!)
  God loves people who live in Timbuktu! (Outrageous love!)
  God loves people who forget to brush their teeth! (Outrageous love!)
  God loves people who are kind! (Outrageous love!)
  God loves people who feel sad! (Outrageous love!)

- Invite the children to share their own statements about God's love, and allow the class to respond.

- **Say:** God wants us to share this outrageous love with other people. One way we can share God's love is by helping people who are in need.

- Invite the children who helped collect the food to report on how much food has been collected so far. Talk about ways to continue encouraging people in your congregation to make gifts of food.

- Ask: What are some other ways that you might share God's love?

- Allow the children an opportunity to discuss their ideas.

Bible Verse Wave

- Ask the children to sit in a circle. Optional: If you have a large class, you can ask the children to sit in rows instead of in a circle and pass the wave from one side of the room to the other and then back.

- Invite the children to say the Bible verse with you.

- **Say:** Now we are going to make things more challenging by adding the wave as we say the Bible verse.

- Choose one child to begin the wave.

- Say: We will say the Bible verse together. As we say the first word, the first person will stand up and raise their arms in the air and then sit down. As we say the second word, the person to their right will stand up and raise their arms in the air and then sit down. The wave will continue around the circle as we say the Bible verse, with one person standing for each word we say.

- Have all the children say the Bible verse as the wave travels around the circle.

- Repeat the activity as the children are interested, trying to get faster with each attempt.

Prepare

✓ Write the Bible verse (John 3:16) on a marker board or a piece of mural paper and place it where it can easily be seen. Depending on the age of your children, you may choose to use only the first part of today's Bible verse.

Small Groups

Divide the children into small groups. You may organize the groups around age levels (4-7, 8-11) or around readers and nonreaders. Keep the groups small, with a maximum of ten children in each group. You may need to have more than one group at each age level.

Prepare

✓ Photocopy Outrageous Ways to Celebrate Christmas (page 47) for each child.

✓ Provide crayons and the Grace Messages cards that you decorated earlier.

Young Children

- Ask: What have you learned about God's love today? (God loves us no matter what. God loves us all the time. God's love is outrageous!) How does it make you feel to know that God loves you so much?

- **Say:** When we know God loves us no matter what, we call that grace. We can't earn grace. God gives it as a gift.

- Show children the Grace Messages cards and read the message.

- **Say:** Some of you helped decorate these cards earlier. When you go home, I'll give each of you a stack of these cards. Hand them out to people you want to share the message of God's grace with. Maybe you know someone who is sad who could especially use a reminder of God's love.

- Ask: Who might you share your cards with?

- Allow the children an opportunity to respond.

- Ask: Why do we celebrate Christmas? (To celebrate the birth of Jesus.)

- **Say:** Since we are celebrating Christmas because God gave us the gift of Jesus, some of the best ways we can celebrate are ways to share love with one another.

- Give each child a copy of Outrageous Ways to Celebrate Christmas (page 47) and a crayon.

- Read the children the paragraph at the top of the page.

- **Say:** As we go through this list, I want you to put a checkmark beside each thing that you would like to do.

- Discuss the items on the list one at a time, asking the children why the idea is a good way to celebrate Christmas. Emphasize that anytime we share love with one another it is a celebration of God's love for us.

- Allow the children to offer ideas to add to the list.

- Have the children write their ideas on the blank lines.

- **Say:** When you go home, hang this note in a place where you will see it and be reminded to do these things.

- **Say:** Before we say our closing prayer, I'll teach you a chant that will help you remember what we've talked about today. First we're going to learn a rhythm pattern to go with the chant. It is two leg pats, three claps, and four snaps.

- Practice the rhythm pattern several times with the children.

- **Say:** Now we will add the words: God gives us a gift—outrageous love!

- Encourage the children to put the rhythm pattern and the words together as follows:

  Two leg pats = God gives
  Three claps = us a gift
  Four snaps = outrageous love

- **Say:** When you go home, you can teach this chant to your family.

- Pray: God, we thank you for your outrageous love for us. Thank you for the gift of Jesus. Help us to remember to share love with others. Amen.

- Give each child some Grace Messages cards to take and share.

Older Children

- Ask: What have you learned about God's love today? (God loves us no matter what. God loves us all the time. God's love is outrageous!)

- **Say:** When we know God loves us no matter what, we call that grace. We can't earn grace. God gives it as a gift.

- Give each child a Grace Messages card and read the message together.

- Ask: How does it make you feel to know that God loves you so much?

- **Say:** Some of you helped decorate these cards earlier. When you go home, I'll give each of you a stack of these cards. Hand them out to people you want to share the message of God's grace with. Maybe you know someone who is sad who could especially use a reminder of God's love.

- Ask: Whom might you share your cards with?

- Allow the children an opportunity to respond.

- Ask: Why do we celebrate Christmas? (To celebrate the birth of Jesus.)

- **Say:** Since the reason we are celebrating Christmas is because God gave us the gift of Jesus, some of the best ways we can celebrate are ways to share love with one another.

- Give each child a copy of Outrageous Ways to Celebrate Christmas (page 47) and a crayon.

- Invite the children to read through the list and check the items they want to do.

Prepare

✓ Photocopy Outrageous Ways to Celebrate Christmas (page 47) for each child.

✓ Provide pencils and the Grace Messages cards that you decorated earlier.

- Ask: Do you think these ideas are good ways to celebrate Christmas? Why or why not?

- Emphasize that anytime we share love with one another, it is a celebration of God's love for us.

- Allow the children to offer ideas to add to the list.

- Have the children write their ideas on the blank lines.

- **Say:** When you go home, hang this note in a place where you will see it and be reminded to do these things.

- **Say:** Before we say our closing prayer, I'll teach you a chant to help you remember what we've talked about today. First we're going to learn a rhythm pattern to go with the chant. It is two leg pats, three claps, and four snaps.

- Practice the rhythm pattern several times with the children.

- **Say:** Now we will add the words: God gives us a gift – outrageous love!

- Encourage the children to put the rhythm pattern and the words together as follows:

  Two leg pats = God gives
  Three claps = us a gift
  Four snaps = outrageous love

- **Say:** When you go home, you can teach this chant to your family.

- Pray: God, we thank you for your outrageous love for us. Thank you for the gift of Jesus. Help us to remember to share outrageous love with everyone we meet. Amen.

- Give each child some Grace Messages cards to take and share.

Grace Messages

 Grace is knowing that God loves you no matter what.

 Grace is knowing that God loves you no matter what.

 Grace is knowing that God loves you no matter what.

 Grace is knowing that God loves you no matter what.

 Grace is knowing that God loves you no matter what.

 Grace is knowing that God loves you no matter what.

 Grace is knowing that God loves you no matter what.

 Grace is knowing that God loves you no matter what.

God's Greatest Gift

God so loved the world that he gave his only Son, so that everyone who believes in him won't perish but will have eternal life.

(John 3:16 CEB)

Outrageous Ways to Celebrate Christmas

At Christmas we celebrate the outrageous love God has for us. God loves us so much God gave us Jesus as the greatest gift of all! We can celebrate God's love for us by sharing outrageous love with others.

I can celebrate Christmas by

❑ spending time with my family.

❑ telling someone God loves them.

❑ drawing a picture for someone.

❑ learning about people who live in another country.

❑ spending time with someone younger than me.

❑ spending time with someone older than me.

❑ helping someone.

❑ telling someone I love them.

❑ _____

❑ _____

❑ _____

4 Jesus' Wish List

Objectives

The children will

- hear Luke 2:8-20;
- learn about the shepherds visiting Jesus;
- discover that Jesus commanded us to love one another;
- explore ways to celebrate Christmas by honoring Jesus' teachings.

Bible Story

The Shepherds Visit Jesus: Luke 2:8-20

Bible Verse

"I give you a new commandment: Love each other. Just as I have loved you, so you also must love each other." (John 13:34 CEB)

Focus for the Teacher

Surprising News

We have heard about the shepherds' visit to Bethlehem so many times that we may fail to realize how surprising and unusual it really was. The term "shepherd" evokes calm, pastoral scenes in our minds. However, at the time Jesus was born, this was far from the case. Shepherding was a despised occupation. Shepherds were on the very fringes of society, looked down upon as shiftless and untrustworthy people. Shepherds often slept outside with their flocks. Imagine how they must have smelled! Yet it was these shepherds who were the first to receive the news of Jesus' birth.

One can imagine that to the shepherds who were used to being looked down upon; the sudden appearance of an angel and then an entire heavenly host must have caused some trembling. The angels, however, had brought good news. In response to this good news, the shepherds hurried off to Bethlehem. The shepherds' response is almost as surprising as the angel's visit. They didn't wait a couple of weeks until they could arrange for someone to watch their sheep so they could take time off. They didn't say, "That's interesting, and next time we're in Bethlehem

we'll check it out." No, the shepherds went "quickly" to find Mary and Joseph and the child of whom they had been told. Once they had seen the baby, the shepherds went and told the news to others. The news was far too wonderful to be kept to oneself!

> The shepherds told others. The news was far too wonderful to be kept to oneself!

The Bible Verse

Today's Bible verse does not come from the Christmas story itself. These words of Jesus, recorded in John 13:34, were spoken to his disciples at the last supper. Jesus' new commandment to his disciples challenges us still today.

Children and Christmas

The story of the shepherds visiting Jesus is one that, like much of the Christmas story, is likely to be familiar to your children. Usually when we teach this story to children, the focus is on the angels appearing and the shepherds rushing off to find Jesus in Bethlehem. These are important aspects of the story, but children may not have thought about what happened after the shepherds found Jesus. As you teach about the shepherds, encourage your children to think about how this event likely changed the shepherds' lives.

Explore Interest Groups

Be sure that adult leaders are waiting when the first child arrives. Greet and welcome each child. Get the children involved in activities that interest them and that introduce the theme for the day's activities.

Food Collection Update

- As the children arrive, have them place any food items they brought in the collection box.

- Have the children check the food collection boxes in other areas of the building and bring the collected food to your classroom, leaving the boxes in place.

- Have the children count the number of items collected. Let them know you will ask them to report on the food drive during large group time.

- **Say:** We will leave the collection boxes in place for one more week and continue encouraging people to bring in food items. Sharing food with others is one way we can show God's love.

Prepare

✓ Place the food collection container near the door.

Bible Verse Puzzle

- **Say:** When Jesus grew up and started teaching, many of the things he taught were different from the teachings people were used to at the time.

- Hand out copies of Jesus' New Commandment (page 57) and encourage the children to complete the puzzle.

Prepare

✓ Photocopy Jesus' New Commandment (page 57) for each child.

✓ Provide pencils or crayons.

Jesus' Wish List

- Show the children the mural paper.

- **Say:** We are making a wish list for Jesus.

- Ask: What do you think Jesus would like for Christmas?

- Write the children's ideas on the list. If children have difficulty coming up with ideas, have them think about what they know about Jesus and the things Jesus taught.

- Give each child a piece of paper.

- Ask: If you could give Jesus anything in the world, what would you choose to give him?

- Encourage each child to draw a picture of a gift for Jesus.

- Display the pictures near Jesus' Wish List.

Prepare

✓ Provide mural paper, drawing paper, crayons, and tape.

✓ Cut a large piece of mural paper and tape it where the children will be able to see it.

✓ At the top of the mural paper, write "Jesus' Wish List."

Continue the Transformation

[Note: If your Nativity set has other barn animal figures, such as donkeys or cows, let the children unwrap them this week also.]

- **Say:** Three weeks ago you transformed a Nativity set by wrapping each piece in fabric, and each week since then we have unwrapped some pieces. We hope that people have seen the Nativity set and have been thinking about it.

- Ask: Do you remember which figures we have unwrapped so far? (Mary, Joseph, angel, and baby Jesus)

- Say: Today we are going to transform the Nativity set again. This time we will unwrap the shepherds and the sheep, while leaving the remaining pieces wrapped.

- Lead the children to where the wrapped Nativity set is on display.

- Have the children unwrap the figures of shepherds and sheep.

- Ask: Do you think anyone will notice this change?

Prepare

✓ Provide poster board and markers.

✓ Look through magazines and cut out some advertisements to show the children as examples.

Design an Ad for Christmas

- Show the children the advertisements you have selected and explain the term "ad."

- Ask: What do these pages have in common? (They are ads trying to get you to buy something or do something.) How do these ads try to get you to use their service or buy their product? (Fun pictures, catchy slogans, bright colors.)

- Ask: If you were going to design an ad for Christmas, what would you include? What do you think is important for people to know about Christmas? Do you think people sometimes get confused about why we celebrate Christmas? Why do you think that happens?

- Have the children work in groups of three or four children each to design a poster advertising Christmas.

- Give each group a piece of poster board and some markers.

- Encourage the children to share their posters with each other.

- Hang the posters up where they can be enjoyed by others in your church.

Make a Table Tent

- Ask: Do you remember what Immanuel means? (God is with us.) Who is called Immanuel? (Jesus.)

- **Say:** We are going to make something you can take home and put on your table to help you remember that God is with you.

- Give the children table tents and have them use markers to write "God is with us" on both sides of the table tent. If you have young children in your class, you may choose to do this step ahead of time.

- Have the children unfold the tents and lay them flat on the table, writing side facing up.

- **Say:** We are going to decorate your table tents by painting with cotton balls.

- Have the children wear art smocks to protect their clothing.

- Give each child a clothespin and a supply of cotton balls.

- Show the children how to put a cotton ball in a clothespin, dip it lightly in paint, and then use it to paint a picture.

- Encourage the children to use a new cotton ball when they change colors.

- Invite the children to decorate their table tents.

- Set the table tents aside to dry until the end of class.

Gather the Flock

- **Say:** In today's Bible story, we are going to hear about shepherds.

- Ask: What do shepherds do? (Take care of sheep.)

- **Say:** Shepherds spent a lot of time in the fields, watching over their sheep while the sheep ate grass. When shepherds needed to move their sheep to another field or into a cave or barn for safety, they would need to gather their sheep all together. We are going to play a silly game pretending that you are shepherds and you need to gather your flock of sheep together. The silly part is that your "sheep" are really going to be water droplets.

- Divide the group into smaller groups of three or four children each.

- Give each group a piece of wax paper and have them spread it out flat on the table or the floor.

- **Say:** I am going to put some water droplet "sheep" on your piece of wax paper. Your job is to gather the "sheep" all together into one "flock." You can do this by using your straw to blow gently on a water droplet and move the droplet where you want it to go. If you blow too hard, you might break your "sheep." You will need to work together with your fellow shepherds to gather all of your sheep.

- Use a medicine-style dropper or a spoon to scatter water droplets on each piece of wax paper.

- Give each child a straw.

- Encourage the children to work together to herd their sheep.

Prepare

✓ Provide cardstock, markers, cotton balls, clothespins, plastic lids, plastic containers, tempera paint, art smocks, and protective table coverings.

✓ Cover the work area and place plastic containers on the table to collect the used cotton balls.

✓ Make paint palettes by putting a few colors of paint in each plastic lid.

✓ Fold the cardstock in half, bringing the long sides together, to form a tent that will stand up.

Prepare

✓ Provide wax paper, water, medicine-style dropper, or spoon and straws.

rge Group

Bring all the children together to experience the Bible story. Use a bell to let the children know large group time is beginning.

Move Like a Shepherd

- **Say:** Our Bible story today will tell us about the shepherds going to Bethlehem to see baby Jesus. Let's pretend that we are shepherds on our way to Bethlehem. However, we won't really move. As we pretend to travel we will stay in one place.

- Give the following directions, encouraging the children to follow the directions while staying in their places.

    Put on your imaginations! We are going to Bethlehem.

    There is a young lamb in your flock that you don't want to leave behind, so you decide to take it along. Pick up the lamb to bring it with you.

    Start walking. Here we go!

    We've come to a steep hill and it's getting harder to walk. Walk as if you are going uphill. Don't drop your lamb!

    The best part of hills is going down the other side. Run down the hill.

    Uh-oh. Here's a stream. Stop and think about how we are going to get to the other side.

    It looks like there are some rocks we can use to cross the stream. Step across on the rocks, being careful not to fall in.

    Whew! That was hard work. Now we can walk again.

    Look! I think I see where the angel told us to go. This is exciting! Let's run the rest of the way. Hold onto your lamb.

    Stop. Here we are. There's the baby in the manger just as the angel said. And there are his mother and father, too.

    Put your lamb down.

    Kneel in front of the manger.

The Shepherds See Jesus

- Ask: Who remembers what book of the Bible our stories have been in the last two weeks? (Luke.)

- **Say:** Today our story again comes from Luke.

- Invite some older children to find Luke 2:8-20 in the Bible.

- Read the Bible story from The Shepherds See Jesus (page 58).

Prepare

✓ Provide Bibles.

✓ Photocopy The Shepherds See Jesus (page 58) for each child to take home.

A Different Kind of Christmas: Children's Leader

- Pause after each section of the story to ask the questions in italics and allow the children to respond.

- **Say:** For the shepherds, seeing Jesus was a life-changing event. They probably never forgot the experience. The Bible tells us they told others what they had seen and heard. Like the shepherds, we know about Jesus. This should make our lives different than they would be if we didn't know about him.

- Ask: How is our celebration of Christmas different because we know about Jesus? (We are celebrating Jesus' birth. The focus is on God's gift to the world.)

Throw Around the Bible Verse

- **Say:** Jesus taught many things about how God wants us to live. Today's Bible verse is one of Jesus' very important lessons.

- Invite some older children to look up John 13:34 and have one of the children read the verse to the class.

- Ask: What does Jesus tell us we are to do? (Love one another.)

- Divide the class into four groups.

- Assign each group a section of the Bible verse and have them practice saying it together a few times.

  Group 1: I give you a new commandment:

  Group 2: Love each other.

  Group 3: Just as I have loved you,

  Group 4: So you also must love each other.

- **Say:** Now we are going to put the verse together. As you say your part of the verse, put your hands in the air and pretend to throw it to the next group. Let's toss around the Bible verse!

- Have the class throw the Bible verse around a few times, trying to make the transitions smooth.

Prepare
✓ Provide Bibles.

Prepare

✓ Bring out Jesus' Wish List from earlier and place it where the children can see it.

✓ Spend some time thinking about possible ministries your class might begin or participate in so that you can offer suggestions if necessary. Ministry needs are different in each congregation and community. You might choose to participate in a project your church is already involved in or you might choose to start a new project. This activity may be a short- or long-term project.

Choose a Class Service Project

- **Say:** Some of you made a wish list for Jesus earlier.

- Read the things on Jesus' Wish List to the class.

- Ask: As you think about our Bible verse today and how Jesus taught that we should love one another, how do you think Jesus would like us to celebrate his birth? (By loving one another.) What are some ways we can show love to one another?

- Allow the children to share their ideas.

- Ask: Is there anything you would add to Jesus' Wish List?

- **Say:** Sharing God's love is a great way to celebrate Christmas. One of the ways we are sharing God's love right now is through our food drive.

- Invite the children who helped collect the food to report on how much food has been collected so far. Talk about ways to continue encouraging people in your congregation to make gifts of food in the next week.

- **Say:** There are many opportunities in our church and our community to do service and share God's love. As a Christmas present for Jesus, our class is going to decide on a service project we can do together.

- Invite the children to come up with ideas for possible ministries that your class could participate in or begin, referring them to Jesus' Wish List for ideas.

- Remind the children that all ideas are welcome.

- As a class, discuss the ideas and choose one you would like to pursue.

- Ask: What would we need to do in order to participate in or begin this ministry? What will we need to do first? What will we need to do next?

- Make a plan to implement your class's ministry project.

- **Say:** Because we know that God sent Jesus as a gift to the world, we respond by finding ways to share God's love.

Small Groups

Divide the children into small groups. You may organize the groups around age levels (4-7, 8-11) or around readers and nonreaders. Keep the groups small, with a maximum of ten children in each group. You may need to have more than one group at each age level.

Young Children

- Ask: What is it we are celebrating at Christmas? (Jesus' birthday. God is with us.)

- Invite the children to think of someone they want to make a gift for.

- **Say:** Think of something they do really well. Maybe they give the best hugs or bake the best cookies. Or maybe they really know how to cheer you up when you're sad or play the best game of tag.

- Allow the children to share their ideas.

- **Say:** You are going to make certificates for these people, declaring that they are the best at whatever you came up with.

- Give each child a certificate (page 59).Invite the children to fill in the name and what the person is best at. Help the younger children as necessary. Have each child sign the certificate.

- Have each child roll up the certificate and secure it with a rubber band. Have each child cut a piece of ribbon and tie it around the certificate. Have each child write the recipient's name on the outside of the present.

- **Say:** These are great presents, because they will let the people know you appreciate them.

- Give each child a paper plate and a napkin.

- Invite each child to use the pretzel shapes to form a Christmas picture, encouraging them to break the pretzels as needed and lay their artwork out on their plate. For example, an angel might be formed by using a circle-shaped pretzel for a head, pretzel sticks for a body, and pretzel twists for wings.

- Encourage the children to admire each other's artwork.

- Enjoy the pretzel snack.

- **Say:** When you go home, remember to tell your family about the service project we are planning to do as a class.

- Pray: God, thank you for the gift of Jesus. Help us to honor you by remembering to love each other as Jesus taught. Amen.

Prepare

✓ Photocopy a certificate (page 59) for each child.

✓ Provide crayons, ribbon, rubber bands, scissors, pretzels in a variety of shapes (twists, rods, circles), paper plates, and napkins.

Prepare

✓ Photocopy a certificate (page 59) for each child.

✓ Provide colored pencils, ribbon, rubber bands, scissors, pretzels in a variety of shapes (twists, rods, circles), paper plates, and napkins.

Older Children

- Ask: What is it that we are celebrating at Christmas? (Jesus' birthday. God is with us.)

- **Say:** Sometimes people spend a lot of money buying presents for other people at Christmas.

- Ask: Can you think of presents you can give that don't cost any money?

- Allow the children time to share their ideas.

- Say: Today we are going to make a present for someone.

- Invite the children to think of someone they want to make a gift for.

- **Say:** Think of something they do really well. Maybe they give the best hugs or bake the best cookies. Or maybe they really know how to cheer you up when you're sad or play the best game of tag.

- Allow the children to share their ideas.

- **Say:** You are going to make a certificate for these people, declaring that they are the best at whatever you came up with.

- Give each child a certificate (page 59). Invite the children to fill in the name and what the person is best at. Have each child sign the certificate.

- Have each child roll up the certificate and secure it with a rubber band. Have each child cut a piece of ribbon and tie it around the certificate. Have each child write the recipient's name on the outside of the present.

- **Say:** These are great presents because they will let the people know you appreciate them.

- Give each child a paper plate and a napkin.

- Invite each child to use the pretzel shapes to form a Christmas picture, encouraging them to break the pretzels as needed and lay their artwork out on their plate. For example, an angel might be formed by using a circle shaped pretzel for a head, pretzel sticks for a body, and pretzel twists for wings.

- Encourage the children to admire each other's artwork.

- Enjoy the pretzel snack.

- **Say:** When you go home, remember to tell your family about the service project we are planning to do as a class.

- Pray: God, thank you for the gift of Jesus. Help us to remember Jesus' teachings as we celebrate his birth. Help us to honor you by remembering to love each other as Jesus taught. Amen.

A Different Kind of Christmas: Children's Leader

Jesus' New Commandment

God sent Jesus into the world to show us the way God wants us to live. Work the puzzle below to discover one of Jesus' most important teachings.

Each line below is missing one letter of the alphabet. Write the missing letter at the end of each line, and then read down to discover what Jesus taught us to do.

ABCDEFGHIJKMNOPQRSTUVWXYZ ____

ABCDEFGHIJKLMNPQRSTUVWXYZ ____

ABCDEFGHIJKLMNOPQRSTUWXYZ ____

ABCDFGHIJKLMNOPQRSTUVWXYZ ____

ABCDFGHIJKLMNOPQRSTUVWXYZ ____

BCDEFGHIJKLMNOPQRSTUVWXYZ ____

ABDEFGHIJKLMNOPQRSTUVWXYZ ____

ABCDEFGIJKLMNOPQRSTUVWXYZ ____

ABCDEFGHIJKLMNPQRSTUVWXYZ ____

ABCDEFGHIJKLMNOPQRSUVWXYZ ____

ABCDEFGIJKLMNOPQRSTUVWXYZ ____

ABCDFGHIJKLMNOPQRSTUVWXYZ ____

ABCDEFGHIJKLMNOPQSTUVWXYZ ____

The Shepherds See Jesus

Based on Luke 2:8-20

Near Bethlehem there were shepherds living in the fields, guarding their sheep at night.

What might you have heard if you had been with the shepherds in the field? What might you have smelled?

•

Suddenly an angel stood before them, and the field around them became bright. They were scared! The angel said, "Don't be afraid! Look! I bring good news to you – wonderful, joyous news for all people. Today in Bethlehem your savior, Christ the Lord, has been born. If you go to Bethlehem, you will find a newborn baby wrapped snugly and lying in a manger." Suddenly a great number of angels were praising God. They said, "Glory to God in heaven, and on earth peace."

What do you think the angels sounded like? How many angels do you think there were? What do you imagine the angels looked like?

When the angels returned to heaven, the shepherds said to each other, "Let's go right now to Bethlehem and see what's happened." They went quickly and found Mary and Joseph, and the baby lying in the manger. They reported what the angel had told them about this child.

How do you think the shepherds felt when they saw that what the angel had told them was true?

•

The shepherds returned home, glorifying and praising God for all they had heard and seen.

What do you think the shepherds said about their experience? How do you think people reacted to their news? Do you think the shepherds ever forgot this experience?

This certificate is awarded to

_____

for being the best

_____

Thank you!

Awarded by:

_____

5 By a Different Road

<table>
<tr><td>

Objectives

The children will
- hear Matthew 2:1-12;
- learn how the wise men honored Jesus;
- discover that loving God means doing God's work;
- explore ways to celebrate Christmas by helping other people.

</td><td>

Bible Story

The Wise Men: Matthew 2:1-12

Bible Verse

This is how everyone will know that you are my disciples, when you love each other. (John 13:35 CEB)

</td></tr>
</table>

Focus for the Teacher

With Joy

The Magi, or wise men, were Gentiles who had traveled from the east. These Magi were non-Jews who came searching for Jesus. They had not been waiting for the birth of the Messiah for hundreds of years, as the Jews had. They came because they were astrologers who had seen a new star. They believed the appearance of a new star meant a new king had been born, and they were curious.

The wise men's search for the new king led them to the current leader, King Herod. There they were directed to Bethlehem by the chief priests and scribes, who shared with them the prophecy of Micah. They also received a request from King Herod to report back to him when they found the one they were looking for.

After their encounter with King Herod, the wise men continued on their journey, following the star that led them to Bethlehem. Luke tells us that when the star stopped, the wise men were "filled with joy" (Luke 2:10). Even though the wise men had not been anticipating the birth of the Messiah as the Jews had, they experienced the same joyful response to Jesus' birth that we saw from the shepherds. The wise men acted on their feelings of joy by worshiping Jesus and by offering him gifts.

The last we hear of the wise men is when they chose to ignore King Herod's request to report back, instead heeding God's warning in a dream and deciding to return home by a different route. The story of the wise men shows that Jesus was born to bring God's love to all people, not just the Jewish people to whom God had promised a Savior.

The Bible Verse

Today's Bible verse (John 13:35) is found right after last week's verse (John 13:34). In verse 34, Jesus gave his disciples the new commandment to love each other. Then in verse 35, as if the disciples had asked why, Jesus went on to explain, "This is how everyone will know that you are my disciples."

Children and Christmas

As this study wraps up, we hope the children in your class have begun to view Christmas as more than a frenzy of writing letters to Santa and unwrapping presents. Children (and adults) find it comforting to know that God is always with us and loves us no matter what. This week, remind the children that even when Christmas celebrations are over, the message of Christmas—that God is with us— lasts all year long.

Explore Interest Groups

Be sure that adult leaders are waiting when the first child arrives. Greet and welcome each child. Get the children involved in activities that interest them and that introduce the theme for the day's activities.

Bible Verse Puzzle

- **Say:** Our Bible verse for today tells us how people will know that we follow Jesus.

- Hand out copies of Starry Message (page 69) and encourage the children to solve the puzzle.

Final Food Count

- As the children arrive, have them place any food items they brought in the collection box.

- Have the children check the food collection boxes in other areas of the building and bring the boxes to your classroom, since today is the last day of the food collection.

- Have the children count the number of items collected. Let them know you will ask them to report on the food drive during large group time.

- Invite the children to use the food items to build something, perhaps a pyramid or a road. Depending on the size of your class and the amount of food collected, you may choose to divide the children into groups for this activity.

- **Say:** We have collected a lot of food! Sharing food with others is one way we can show God's love. This food will be appreciated by those who receive it.

Final Transformation

- **Say:** At the beginning of this study you transformed a Nativity set by wrapping each piece in fabric, and each week since then we have unwrapped some pieces. We hope that people have seen the Nativity set and have been thinking about it.

- Ask: Do you remember which figures are still wrapped up? (The wise men.)

- **Say:** Today we are going to finish unwrapping the Nativity set.

- Lead the children to where the wrapped Nativity set is on display.

- Have the children unwrap the figures of the wise men.

- Ask: Do you think anyone will notice that the Nativity set is completely unwrapped now?

Prepare

✓ Photocopy Starry Message (page 69) for each child.

✓ Provide pencils or crayons.

Prepare

✓ Place the food collection container near the door.

✓ Arrange for the food to be taken to the place where you are delivering it after this class.

Prepare

✓ Provide dark-colored construction paper, cotton-tipped swabs, salt, water, and small glasses.

✓ Before class, make a super-saturated salt solution by heating water in a small pan, then adding salt and stirring to dissolve. Continue adding salt until no more salt will dissolve. You should be able to dissolve approximately 1/4-cup salt in 1 cup of water. Pour the salt solution into small glasses and cool to room temperature. It is fine if some salt settles on the bottom.

Prepare

✓ Provide refrigerated biscuit dough (one can for each eight children), jelly or jam (one or more kinds), cookie sheets, and spoons.

✓ Preheat an oven to 400 degrees.

Crystal Pictures

- Show the children the glasses of solution.

- Ask: Do you have any ideas about what might be in these glasses?

- **Say:** It looks kind of like water, but it is special water because I have dissolved salt in it. We are going to use this special solution to paint with. As the pictures dry, the water will evaporate and leave sparkly salt crystals behind on the paper.

- Give each child a piece of dark construction paper and a cotton-tipped swab.

- Show the children how to dip the end of the swab in the solution and then draw on their paper. Encourage the children to re-wet the swab frequently.

- Invite the children to make designs such as stars, spirals, and polka dots on their paper.

- Invite the children to spell their name on the paper.

- Set the papers aside to dry.

Make jelly-topped Biscuits

- **Say:** We are going to make a special snack that we can enjoy during our small group time today.

- Have the children wash their hands.

- Have the children open the cans of refrigerated biscuit dough and place the biscuits about 2 inches apart on ungreased cookie sheets.

- Have the children carefully spread each biscuit wider so that an indentation forms in the center, being careful not to create a hole through the biscuit.

- Have the children place a spoonful of jelly or jam in the center of each biscuit.

- Bake the biscuits for 10 to 12 minutes until golden brown.

- Let the biscuits cool until small group time.

What Is Different?

- Provide a variety of dress-up items such as colorful scarves, hats, sunglasses, and belts.

- **Say:** We have been talking for several weeks about different ways to celebrate Christmas. Today we are going to play a game to see how good you are at noticing differences.

- Choose three children to begin the game. Invite them to dress up using the items provided. Each child may use several items.

- When the children are finished, ask them to stand in front of the other children and model their outfits.

- **Say:** Take a good look so you can remember how each child is dressed.

- Lead the three children out of the area, and have them each change one thing about their appearance. For example, a child may change to a different-colored scarf or take off their sunglasses or add a belt.

- Lead the children back into the area, and invite them to model their outfits once more. Ask the rest of the children to figure out what is different about each child.

- When all the changes have been guessed, choose three more children to dress up.

- If the game becomes too easy, have the models change multiple things about their outfits.

Roving Reporter

- Invite several older children to be roving reporters.

- Ask: Do you know what roving reporters are? (People who roam around, watching and interviewing, then report what they have seen and heard.)

- **Say:** We have been talking about Christmas for several weeks now. I would like you to wander around during this activity time and watch what is going on. You may also interview some people.

- Ask: What are some questions we could ask to discover what people have learned the last few weeks?

- Working together, have the children come up with several questions such as "Why do we celebrate Christmas? What Christmas celebration helps you remember God is with you? How do you show God's love to others at Christmastime?"

- Give each of the children a pencil, along with a small notebooks or a clipboard with paper. Ask the children to use the questions in their jobs as roving reporters. Tell them you will ask them later to report on what they find out.

Prepare

✓ Provide a pencil for each child, along with a small notebook or a clipboard with paper.

Large Group

Bring all the children together to experience the Bible story. Use a bell to call them to large group time.

Here's What's Happening

- **Say:** You might have noticed that some of your friends have been walking around asking questions today. I asked them to act as roving reporters and to find out what was happening this morning and what you have learned during the last few weeks. Let's hear their reports.

- Invite the reporters to tell what they have learned by watching and asking questions.

- **Say:** Today is also the last day of our food drive.

- Have the children admire the food sculptures.

- Invite the children who counted the food to share how much food has been collected.

- **Say:** I can see that you all know what Christmas is about.

Prepare

✓ Photocopy Visitors from Far Away (page 70) for each child.

✓ Provide Bibles.

Visitors From Far Away

- **Say:** We have been talking about the Christmas story for several weeks now.

- Ask: What parts of the Christmas story have we talked about so far?

- Allow the children to share what they remember about the Christmas story.

- Ask: Do you know any parts of the Christmas story we haven't talked about yet?

- **Say:** You're right! We haven't talked about the wise men, or Magi. That is what our Bible story is about today. The story of the Magi is found in the gospel of Matthew.

- Invite some older children to find Matthew 2:1-12 in the Bible.

- **Say:** In our story today, the wise men are called Magi. Regardless of whether we call them wise men or Magi, we know they traveled from far away to find Jesus. As you listen to today's story, every time you hear the word "Magi" I want you to say "visitors from far away." Let's see if you are good listeners.

- Read the Bible story in Visitors from Far Away (page 70), pausing each time after the word Magi to let the children respond.

- Ask: Why did King Herod ask the Magi to come back and tell him when they found the baby? (He was afraid. He wanted to harm Jesus.) Did the Magi do what Herod asked? (No, they went home by a different road.) Why not? (God warned them in a dream not to return to Herod.)

Say: Like the shepherds, the Magi were changed by seeing Jesus. They honored him with gifts, and then they listened to the message God gave them in a dream.

• Ask: How does our life change by knowing about Jesus? (We try to follow his teachings.)

• **Say:** At Christmas we celebrate that God sent Jesus into the world. This is something we need to remember not only at Christmas, but all the time.

• Write the Bible verse on the marker board: This is how everyone will know that you are my disciples, when you love each other. (John 13:35 CEB)

Show and tell

• Ask: How many of you know what show and tell is?

• **Say:** Today we are going to do an activity that's a little bit different. First we are going to tell, and then we are going to show.

• Invite one of the children to come forward, and show that child one of the objects under the towel without letting the rest of the class see.

• **Say:** Without telling you what the item is, _____ is going to describe to you what is underneath this towel. As you hear the description, try to imagine in your mind what the object looks like.

• Invite the child to describe the object. Offer encouragement and ask questions to assist as necessary.

• Ask: Do you think you know what this object looks like?

• Have the child show the object to the class.

• Ask: Is this what you thought it would look like? How is it different than you imagined?

• Repeat the game several times, inviting different children to describe each object.

• Ask: Is it easier to know what an object looks like when you are told about it or when you see it? (When you see it.) Why?

• **Say:** Jesus tells us that we are to show other people God's love. Then we are to tell them that God loves them. Show and tell. Our Bible verse today reminds us that when we show love to each other, people will know we are followers of Jesus.

Prepare

✓ Provide a variety of objects for the children to describe, such as a picture frame, a stuffed animal, a Christmas ornament, a plant, and a book.

✓ Place the items out of sight under a towel.

Small Groups

Divide the children into small groups. You may organize the groups around age levels (4-7, 8-11) or around readers and nonreaders. Keep the groups small, with a maximum of ten children in each group. You may need to have more than one group at each age level.

Prepare

✓ Provide paper, crayons, markers, colored pencils, paper lunch bags, ribbon, scissors, paper punches, paper plates, and napkins.

✓ Place the biscuits baked earlier on plates for each small group.

Young Children

- Say: Over the last five weeks, we have talked about the Christmas story, God being with us always, God's gift of Jesus, and ways we can share God's love with the world.

- Ask: What do you remember about the things we've talked about?

- Allow the children an opportunity to share.

- Say: Today we are going to make one more present for you to take home and share with your family.

- Hand out paper to the children and encourage them to write something they know about Christmas that they consider good news. Some examples include: "Jesus is God's gift to the world!" "God is with us!" and "God loves me no matter what!"

- Encourage the children to decorate their papers.

- Give the children paper lunch bags and invite them to decorate the bags.

- Have the children fold up the good news messages and place them inside the decorated lunch bags.

- Have the children fold over about two inches of the top of the lunch bags.

- Have the children use paper punches to punch two holes in each folded-over portion of the paper bags.

- Have the children cut one piece of ribbon each, about 9 inches long.

- Have the children put the ribbon through the holes in the paper bag and tie the ends together in a bow.

- Say: You have made a gift of good news to share with your family. When they open it, tell them why you chose the good news message you did.

- Give each child a paper plate and a napkin.

- Share a snack of the biscuits made earlier.

- As the group eats, discuss the progress of the class service project planned last week. If you have already completed it, ask about the children's experiences. If the project is still in the planning process, discuss how the planning is progressing.

A Different Kind of Christmas: Children's Leader

- Say: When you go home, talk to your family about planning and doing a service project together. Think about ways you can show and tell God's love together as a family.

- Pray: Loving God, we thank you for the good news we remember at Christmas. Help us to remember this good news all year. Amen.

Older Children

- Say: Over the last five weeks, we have talked about the Christmas story, God being with us always, God's gift of Jesus, and ways we can share God's love with the world.

- Ask: What do you remember about the things we've talked about?

- Allow the children an opportunity to share.

- Say: Today we are going to make one more present for you to take home and share with your family.

- Hand out paper to the children and encourage them to write something they know about Christmas that they consider good news. Some examples include: "Jesus is God's gift to the world! God is with us!" and "God loves me no matter what!"

- Encourage the children to write "This is good news because . . . " and finish the sentence.

- Encourage the children to decorate their papers.

- Give the children paper lunch bags and invite them to decorate the bags.

- Have the children fold up the good news messages and place them inside the decorated lunch bags.

- Have the children fold over about two inches of the top of each lunch bag.

- Have the children use paper punches to punch two holes in the folded-over portion of each paper bag.

- Have the children cut pieces of ribbon about 9 inches long.

- Have the children put the ribbon through the holes in the paper bags and tie the ends together in a bow.

- Say: You have made a gift of good news to share with your family.

Prepare

✓ Provide paper, crayons, markers, colored pencils, paper lunch bags, ribbon, scissors, paper punches, paper plates, and napkins.

✓ Place the biscuits baked earlier on plates for each small group.

When they open it, tell them why you chose the good news message that you did.

- Give each child a paper plate and a napkin. Share a snack of the biscuits made earlier.

- As you are eating, discuss the progress of the class service project planned last week. If you have already completed it, ask about the children's experiences. If the project is still in the planning process, discuss how the planning is progressing.

- Say: When you go home, talk to your family about planning and doing a service project together. Think about ways you can show and tell God's love together as a family.

- Pray: Loving God, we thank you for the good news we remember at Christmas. Help us to remember to share this good news with others by showing your love and telling people about you. Amen.

Starry Message

Each word below has stars beneath it. Beginning with the word that has only one star beneath it, and going in order until you find the word with sixteen stars beneath it, write each word in order on the lines below. When you are finished, you will see a message Jesus had for his disciples. You can check your answer by looking up John 13:35 (CEB).

love
★★★★★★★★★★★
★★★★

know
★★★★★★

when
★★★★★★★★★★★★★★
★★

you
★★★★★★★★

that
★★★★★★★

how
★★★

is
★★

you
★★★★★★★★★★★★★
★★★

another
★★★★★★★★★★★
★★★★★★

will
★★★★★

disciples
★★★★★★★★★★★
★

This
★

my
★★★★★★★★★★★★

are
★★★★★★★★★★

everyone
★★★★

one
★★★★★★★★★★★
★★★★★

_____

_____

_____

Visitors From Far Away

Based on Matthew 2:1-12

After Jesus was born in Bethlehem, some Magi (visitors from far away) came to Jerusalem. These men were astrologers who studied the stars. They had seen a new star and believed this meant a new king had been born. The Magi (visitors from far away) arrived in Jerusalem asking, "Where is the child who has been born king of the Jews? We'd like to find him so we can worship him."

Now, when King Herod heard what the Magi (visitors from far away) were asking, he was frightened. He was afraid that a new king would be a threat to him as the current ruler. He called together his advisors and asked them what they knew about the birth of a Messiah. The chief priests told King Herod that the Messiah would be born in Bethlehem because that was what had been foretold.

When King Herod heard this news, he called for the Magi (visitors from far away) and asked them to tell him everything they knew about the star. Then he sent the Magi (visitors from far away) to Bethlehem to find the child. Before the Magi (visitors from far away) left, King Herod told them, "When you find the child, let me know. I would like to worship him, too." Although the Magi (visitors from far away) didn't know it at the time, King Herod was lying. He didn't really want to worship Jesus; he wanted to harm him.

The Magi (visitors from far away) left King Herod and continued on their journey, traveling by night and following the star. The star led them to Bethlehem where it stopped over a house. When the wise men saw that the star had stopped, they were filled with joy. They went into the house and found the child, Jesus, with his mother, Mary. They knelt down and worshiped Jesus. The Magi (visitors from far away) had brought gifts to honor the new king: gold, frankincense, and myrrh.

The Magi (visitors from far away) remembered that King Herod had asked them to report back to him, but God warned them in a dream that this was a bad idea. Instead, they returned to their country by a different route.